Garry's Notes

Introduction

The purpose of this written project was at first, a way to put all my notes together of which, I have collected over time. Information and web links which are in this collection can be found by doing your own research and spending a lot of time in review. My notes are here to provide you with a quick and no-nonsense way to figure out if you would like to become a miner using cloud services. It's written in a short story format. I'm no expert, but as a digital coin cryptocurrency miner/hobbyist, I think this information could be beneficial to others such as you as well. It's not meant to be a Digital coin bible but a quick and easy reference, with most everything you might need to know to get started. I say most, because we are always learning more each and every day. So, to make things easy to read about and to give you some options, I have sorted the notes into many chapters. Some of these chapters may wander a bit as I tell my side of the story in mining cryptocurrency/digital coins in the cloud without hardware. It takes about 45 minutes or less, to read all the way through.

Please forgive me if I don't set this book up in a collegian format. References are given at the best of my knowledge at the end of the book. I will always give credit to the writer/researcher. Lord knows, I didn't come up with all the data on my own. Much of this e book was found as is, where it is, on the web. It's a collection of all my notes, compressed and edited for content to share with you. I'm also the author of Quail Notes and my writing format is very similar to that E book and Printed book. There's so much out there, and much of the info I'm going to share, has no author. If you have read some or most of this before, just skip to the parts that interest you. You won't hurt my feelings. The reference to all the notes from the web are posted as a link in front of the article. And reposted again at the back of my notes.

Sit back and let me tell you a story about my Digital mining experience.

About me

I'd like to say, this collection of digital coin notes isn't about me really, but about mining for the many types of coins in the cloud. Specifically about the way I go about mining for them and my experiences while doing this. My favorite so far is EoBot. These notes are mostly about my experience with them.

There are many cloud based coin miners out there and I can't say I have experienced them all. I have experienced a few of them and I'm only going to share about how basically one of them works. I will on occasion give reference to the others from time to time to compare them as I tell you my side of the story.

I was raised in the USA, state of Oklahoma, out in the country near a town called Wayne. I only mention this, because so many readers that are interested in mining for digital coins are from all over the world. Back then we didn't have the internet or digital TV or even cable. We had 3 free channels to watch our shows, news or weather. Hasn't our world changed in the past 20 years? Some of my family still lives just far enough away from the city that a connection to the World Wide Web is limited by the distance or the speed of the satellite connection or line of sight tower connections. Trying to mine with hardware at home on these electronic devices is impossible. Mining for digital currency not only needs the fastest hardware, but a solid high speed internet connection that's reliable. I'm currently living and working in Hawaii, on the island of Kauai. My internet speed is nice at 15 Megs per second download and 0.3 Megs per second uploading. But the electrical costs run an average of .0.57 cents per kilowatt compared to many other less expensive locations which might only cost 0.04 cents per kilowatt in Oklahoma and Texas. My connection also fails at least 12 times a day, even for a few seconds. We also lose power or the power will blink every few days, resulting with most computer devices having to be reset These are some of the reasons I have become interested in digital coin mining in the cloud. With hardware costs, internet down time, electrical fees and more, there's no other way I could do it.

Let's looks at the web and get a bit of information about Bitcoins. All links to the web versions have been included, so you can research that article in more depth for yourself or group if needed.

Questions on the web:

What is Bitcoin?

Bitcoin is a new form of digital currency, designed for the Internet. It is completely decentralized, and is not controlled by any government entities. The easiest way to think about the Bitcoin is that it is a global ledger of accounts.

Does someone control the Bitcoin network?

No single person or entity owns the Bitcoin network. Bitcoin is controlled by every Bitcoin user worldwide. For example, as developers improve the underlying Bitcoin software, they must propose the changes to the network, and there must be unanimous consensus among all users to implement those changes. This gives Bitcoin users and developers the incentive to strive for consensus.

How does Bitcoin work?

Bitcoin can be boiled down to two distinct components: a user-friendly wallet application that allows users to send and receive Bitcoin, and the Bitcoin Core, which provides the infrastructure for these transactions to occur.

Behind the scenes, the Bitcoin network shares the "block chain", which is a distributed ledger. It contains every transaction since the beginning of Bitcoin, and allows a user's computer to verify the validity of each transaction. Each transaction's authenticity is protected by digital signatures corresponding to the sending addresses. Transactions are processed by "mining", which is essentially using the computational power of specialized hardware to store transactions in the blockchain.

Where can I use Bitcoin?

You can use Bitcoin at thousands of online retail stores, as well as many restaurants, food delivery services, and of course, mining hardware companies. You can now trade

Bitcoin on Coinbase's new regulated US exchange, which operates in 25 states.

Some of the most famous companies that accept Bitcoin include Microsoft, Dell, Overstock, Newegg, PayPal (via BrainTree), Foodler, Virgin Galactic, WordPress, TigerDirect, Tesla, Zynga, and thousands of others.

Mining Questions

What is Bitcoin Mining?

Mining is the act of helping the Bitcoin network record transactions in a provable way. Without getting into the details of the SHA256 algorithm, mining is helping the Bitcoin network by recording transactions in the distributed ledger, and in exchange for miners' computing power, miners are rewarded with Bitcoin. This is our goal.

The easiest way to describe the Bitcoin network is to think of it as a distributed ledger of account balances, denominated in Bitcoin. We refer to a Bitcoin account as an "address," which is a unique string of letters and numbers that references a specific account. The ledger of accounts we mentioned includes not only a complete list of accounts (addresses), as well as their current balance, but every transaction that has occurred since day one. We say it is distributed because it is stored on thousands of computers around the world, which provides redundancy against any single point of failure. While one person, region or country could be disconnected from the network, Bitcoin is functional as long as there are 2 or more instances of the software running.

Transactions between addresses are stored incrementally, approximately every 10 minutes. We call these incremental lists of transactions "blocks." Each block must reference the previous block before it, resulting in a chain of blocks known as the blockchain. The blockchain is essentially the Bitcoin network's database that stores a record of every transaction, dating all the way back to the original Genesis block. Bitcoins ONLY exist in the blockchain, so clearly we need to verify that the blockchain is not only accurate, but secure against attack or fraud. This is where mining comes in, which secures the transactions in the ledger.

More about BITCOIN MINING

Think of mining as a globally distributed security system for Bitcoin. Mining is the process of encapsulating all of the most recent transactions into a new block of transactions, which must fulfill a number of specific rules. First, in order for a mined block to be considered permanent, it must refer to the previous block before it. Second, it must include as many transactions to date as possible. Third, it must fulfill a very complex mathematical equation. The mathematical equation involves "hashing" long strings of letters and numbers using the SHA-256 algorithm to generate a very large number. Once this calculation is performed, and submitted to the network, this is considered a "hash". Most hardware routinely performs billions or trillions of these calculations per second. The miner who provides the best solution to a given block, which satisfies all three requirements, receives a reward of 25 Bitcoins! Bitcoin mining evolved from using personal computers that were able to process thousands of these calculations per second to Bitcoin-specific chips that can process billions of SHA-256 hashes per second.

An important point to mention is that production of Bitcoin is designed to decrease over time, which means the Bitcoin block reward will decrease by half every four years. As of early 2015, approximately 13.5 million Bitcoins have been produced. There is a limit of 21 million Bitcoins that will be produced before the year 2140, which means 64% of the world Bitcoin supply has already been created. The next "halving day" is expected at the end of 2016, when the award will be cut in half, to 12.5 Bitcoins per block.

What kind of hardware do I need to mine Bitcoins?

At this point, Application Specific Integrated Circuits (ASICs) are required to mine. Some hardware manufacturers produce miners with a single high-powered chip, while many others produce systems that incorporate many smaller chips all mining in tandem. If you wanted to mine Bitcoins at home, you would need a hardware-based miner from a manufacturer such as Bitmain or Spondoolies, to name just a few.

What is cloud mining? (Our interest)

Cloud mining takes the same concepts used in cloud computing, and applies them to Bitcoin mining. Rather than hosting a website, an email service or a file sharing service in the cloud, cloud Bitcoin mining companies will mine Bitcoins for users. Companies will purchase, host, and maintain the hardware at massive data centers, and provide specified amounts of hash rate (mining power) to clients, for a fee. Hash rate is usually described in terms of GH/S (gigahashes per second) or TH/S (terahashes per second).

Big Question of the Day. Is cloud mining profitable?

That depends on a number of factors that contribute to a contract's return on investment or ROI. Cost is an obvious factor, which is why the rating criteria revolved heavily around price. Maintenance fees cover electricity, hosting, and maintenance of hardware, and can eat into profits, so all other things being equal, these two factors are the most important to consider when determining profitability. However, the reputation and track record of a company is incredibly important, because of the prevalence of ponzi schemes and bankruptcies in the Bitcoin mining space. ROI can become impossible if your 5 year contract is terminated after 2 months. Finally, profitability comes down to the 2 factors that no single company can predict or control. Bitcoin's price has fluctuated all over the map, from pennies to over $1000 and back to under $200 in the space of 3 years. At the time of this writing, it's at $246.42 However, when purchasing a mining contract, it is best to assume a constant price for Bitcoin, since your alternative is to simply purchase Bitcoin and hold it, hoping for a price increase. The other factor that impacts mining in a very big way is Bitcoin network difficulty. Difficulty is determined by global hash rate, which was increasing at an exponential rate until late 2014, when it began to plateau. Whether this plateau continues will likely depend on the price of Bitcoin, as well as innovations in ASIC development.

A few Cloud Miners that you can check out.

Cloudmirr.io

GAW Miners, ZenMiner, Zencloud

PBMining was determined to be a MINING PONZI SCHEME

Genesis Mining

HashNest

EoBot Mining.   It's **my favorite** so far.   Follow this link to see my cloud miner at work. You're welcome to save this link for viewing at any time. No need for a bitcoin wallet to begin with, but you will need one soon. They will accept PayPal and your cloud miner experience can begin in less than 3 minutes. I convert my income into more Hash power about once a week. If my cryptocurrency value is very low, it's because I have traded the income into a higher hash rate. Please follow my live page. You can see it mining and observe the speed and the types of coins I'm currently mining live.

https://www.eobot.com/user/158433

There are many more online cloud based E coin miners out there. Just do your homework and beware of those that are pyramid based. Make sure your choice has real functioning hardware for mining. Ease of use interface should be functional and aesthetic to the eye. Most all cloud miners require electronic coins to begin. You will need a bitcoin wallet for most cloud miners. A few can accept PayPal in addition to bitcoins. EoBot is one of those companies which allow PayPal to be used. Digital wallets aren't needed to get started, but is recommended. PayPal has a 180 day restriction on this type of purchase before you're allowed to withdraw any profits from mining. You're not able to collect e coins from EoBot or any other profits due to these regulations. I see it as a 5 year plan, and a180 day (6 months) hold on returning profits, doesn't affect my goal. I'm looking for a decent ROI (Return On Investment). Please be aware of bitcoin faucets and others which may or may not be attempts to get your email for spam. There are also, web sites that offer bitcoins for clicking on links, playing games (0.0015 cents a day on average) and a large number of them pay a very small royalty for referring new client's to them. I'm sure the ratios of bitcoin faucets outnumber the real online cloud miners 1000 to 1.

Most, if not all of the cloud miners will post a warning that they don't allow fiat moneys in or out (fiat is the term for real cash). New banking and government rules and regulations would limit their use. Many are based in countries that are less limited in regulations in this type of financial use. Thus, all payouts in all cloud miners are e coin based. You're paying for leased computer hash power and it's not really an investment with an income (per say).

Note to everyone: Cloud mining should be considered as a fun, recreational activity and not a source of income or investment. If you're mining or just trading bitcoins, the market is always high risk.

More from the web:

http://en.m.wikipedia.org/wiki/Bitcoin

dministration Decentralized[note 1]

Date of introduction	3 January 2009; 6 years ago
User(s)	Worldwide
Supply growth	25 bitcoins per block (approximately every ten minutes) until mid 2016,[2] and then afterwards 12.5 bitcoins per block for 4 years until next halving. This halving continues until 2110-2140 when 21 million bitcoins have been issued.

Subunit

10^{-3}	millibitcoin
10^{-6}	microbitcoin, bit[3]
10^{-8}	satoshi[4]

Symbol	BTC, [note 2] XBT, [note 3] ₿[note 4]
⬚millibitcoin	mBTC
⬚ microbitcoin, bit[3]	μBTC
Coins	unspent outputs of transactions denominated in any multiple of satoshis[10]:ch. 5

Important Note about Mining Bitcoins of any type.

If you were to understand one thing about the future of bitcoin mining, the system is setup for a maximum bitcoin payout of 21 million coins. At that time, once all the coins have been mined, there are no more. It will become supply and demand. The value of the coin will grow as its use and value increases. If it continues to grow as it has in the past, you should know that there's never a promise of future increases in the market, just speculation. This is the same for all types of digital coins. We as miners can only hope for a continuing bull market. Remember these words from the stock market, bulls climb stairs, but bears fall from windows. It's the same for the e coin market of digital currency, it's up and down.

http://www.butterflylabs.com/bitcoin-mining/

Perhaps the best way to describe Bitcoin mining to the layman would be to say that it is somewhat like a cross between the California Gold Rush and the lottery. No one is given Bitcoins per se. You've got to earn them through mining on hardware or in the cloud. At the same time, you need a little luck. No one can precisely define how long it will take to successfully mine a Bitcoin. While your chances should become better with the more hashes you can generate, there is not always a direct correlation between the amount of work you put in and the rate of success you are going to have. If you're mining as a single miner, your opportunity to get the logical answer before and faster than the 1,000's of others is a serious competition. Most if not all miners join together in a powerful computing pool and they share the rewards based on hash power and the amount of time your setup provides in relation to the other pool miners in the group. You are paid in fractions of the reward.

Bitcoins are a new currency, and they work on a peer-to-peer system, so there is inherent value in their relative scarcity, as well as its independence of a "central authority."

Bitcoin mining becomes more difficult over time, in order to facilitate limitation on the supply. It is referred to as a "high performance computing problem" and thus is best solved with hardware that is specifically built for that purpose. In order to mine Bitcoins, you have to "solve a block," and that gets harder as the network of miners grows. Proof of work must be shown for anything to be valid. It is a very competitive endeavor. To help improve the odds for success, miners often form pools, where resources are combined and any yield from the effort is divided.

Aside from uncovering Bitcoins, which brings its own reward, miners have another incentive; namely, the fees they can collect for transactions on the part of users. The miner rigs are rented out, so they are motivated to include transactions in their block. This becomes a more important factor as the difficulty in creating new Bitcoins increases.

Cloud mining, it's a cutting edge and a ground floor opportunity for everyone. It's clearly no wonder why so many people are excited by Bitcoins! I know I am!

Remember. Its risk versus reward.

Now, a little bit more history of mining:

http://www.bitcoinmining.com/bitcoin-mining-hardware/

Bitcoin mining hardware has evolved dramatically since 2009

At first, miners used their central **processing unit** (CPU) to mine, but soon this wasn't fast enough and it bogged down the system resources of the host computer. Miners quickly moved on to using the **graphical processing unit** (GPU) in computer graphics cards because they were able to hash data 50 to 100 times faster and consumed much less power per unit of work. During the winter of 2011, a new industry sprang up with custom equipment that pushed the performance standards even higher. The first wave of these specialty bitcoin mining devices were produced by <u>Butterfly Labs</u>. These easy to use miners were based on field-programmable gate array (FPGA) processors and attached to computers using a convenient USB connection. FPGA miners used much less power than CPU's or GPU's and made concentrated mining farms possible for the first time.

Today's modern bitcoin mining hardware

Application-specific integrated circuit (ASIC) miners have taken over completely. These ASIC machines mine at unprecedented speeds while consuming much less power than FPGA or GPU mining rigs. Several reputable companies have established themselves with excellent.

Bitcoin Mining Hardware

CPU's: In the beginning, mining with a CPU was the only way to mine bitcoins. Mining this way via the original Satoshi client is how the bitcoin network started. This method is no longer viable now that the network difficulty level is so high. You might mine for years and years without earning a single coin.

GPU's: Soon it was discovered that high end graphics cards were much more efficient at bitcoin mining and the landscape changed. CPU bitcoin mining gave way to the GPU (Graphical Processing Unit). The massively parallel nature of some GPUs allowed for a 50x to 100x increase in bitcoin mining power while using far less power per unit of work. While any modern GPU can be used to mine, the AMD line of GPU architecture turned out to be far superior to the nVidia architecture for mining bitcoins and the ATI Radeon HD 5870 turned out to be the most cost effective choice at the time.

FPGA's: As with the CPU to GPU transition, the bitcoin mining world progressed up the technology food chain to the Field Programmable Gate Array. With the successful launch of the Butterfly Labs FPGA 'Single', the bitcoin mining hardware landscape gave way to specially manufactured hardware dedicated to mining bitcoins. While the FPGAs didn't enjoy a 50x - 100x increase in mining speed as was seen with the transition from CPUs to

GPUs, they provided a benefit through power efficiency and ease of use. A typical 600 MH/s graphics card consumed upwards of 400w of power, whereas a typical FPGA mining device would provide a hashrate of 826 MH/s at 80w of power. That 5x improvement allowed the first large bitcoin mining farms to be constructed at an operational profit. The bitcoin mining industry was born.

ASIC's: The bitcoin mining world is now solidly in the Application Specific Integrated Circuit (ASIC) era. An ASIC is a chip designed specifically to do one thing and one thing only. Unlike FPGA's, an ASIC cannot be repurposed to perform other tasks. An ASIC designed to mine bitcoins can only mine bitcoins and will only ever mine bitcoins. The inflexibility of an ASIC is offset by the fact that it offers a 100x increase in hashing power while reducing power consumption compared to all the previous technologies. For example, a good bitcoin miner like the Monarch from Butterfly Labs provides 600 GH/s (1 Gigahash is 1000 Megahash. 1 GH/s = 1000 MH/s) while consuming 350w of power. Compared to the GPU era, this is an increase in hashrate and power savings of nearly 300x. (Calculate the earnings of any bitcoin mining hardware device using this bitcoin mining calculator).

Bitcoin mining hardware list: Mining hardware comparison

Unlike all the previous generations of hardware preceding ASIC, ASIC is the "end of the line" when it comes to disruptive technology. CPUs were replaced by GPUs which were in turn replaced by FPGAs which were replaced by ASICs. There is nothing to replace ASICs now or even in the immediate future. There will be stepwise refinement of the ASIC products and increases in efficiency, but nothing will offer the 50x - 100x increase in hashing power or 7x reduction in power usage that moves from previous technologies offered. This makes power consumption on an ASIC device the single most important factor of any ASIC product, as the expected useful lifetime of an ASIC mining device is longer than the entire history of bitcoin mining. It is conceivable that an ASIC device purchased today would still be mining in two years if the device is power efficient enough and the cost of electricity does not exceed its output. Mining profitability is also dictated by the exchange rate, but under all circumstances the more power efficient the mining device, the more profitable it is.

Software

There are two basic ways to mine: On your own or as part of a pool. Almost all miners choose to mine on a pool because it takes the luck out of the process. Before you join a pool, make sure you have a bitcoin wallet so you have a place to store your bitcoins. Next you need to join a mining pool like Eclipse, Eligius or BTC Guild. With pool mining, the profit from any block a member generates is divided up among the members of the pool. This gives the pool members a more frequent, steady payout (this is called reducing your variance), but your payout(s) will be less unless you use a zero fee pool like Eclipse. Solo mining will give you large, infrequent payouts and pooled mining will give you small, frequent payouts, but both add up to the same amount if you're using a zero fee pool.

Once you have your client set up or you have registered with a pool, the next step is to set up the actual mining software. The most popular GPU/FPGA/ASIC miner at the moment is BFGminer or CGminer. For a full GUI experience, try EasyMiner.

If you want a quick taste of mining without installing any software, try either EoBot or Bitcoin Plus. Bit coin Plus is also a browser-based CPU Bitcoin miner. As a CPU miner it's not cost-efficient for serious mining, but it does illustrate the principle of pooled mining very well. It's fun with a small $10 start to gain some experience.

http://www.bitcoinmining.com/bitcoin-mining-software/

While the actual process of mining is handled by the mining hardware itself, special software is needed to connect your miners to the blockchain and your mining pool as well, if you are part of a mining pool. The software delivers the work to the miners and receives the completed work from the miners and relays that information back to the blockchain and your mining pool. The software can run on almost any operating system, such as OSX, Windows, Linux, and has even been ported to work on a Raspberry Pi with some modifications for drivers depending on your mining setup.

Not only does the software relay the input and output of your miners to the blockchain, but it also monitors them and displays general statistics such as the temperature, hashrate, fan speed, and average speed of the miner.

There are a few different types of mining software out there and each have their own advantages and disadvantages, so be sure to read up on the various mining software out there.

A few examples of mining software:

EASYMINER: A GUI based miner for Windows, Linux and Android. EasyMiner acts as a convenient wrapper for the built in CG & BFGminer softwares. It auto configures your miners and provides performance graphs to for easy visualization of your mining activity. Download: http://www.butterflylabs.com/drivers/

BFGMINER: A modular ASIC, FPGA, GPU and CPU miner written in C, cross platform for Linux, Mac, and Windows including support for OpenWrt-capable routers.
Download: https://github.com/luke-jr/bfgminer

CGMINER: This is a multi-threaded multi-pool GPU, FPGA and ASIC miner with ATI GPU monitoring, (over)clocking and fanspeed support for bitcoin and derivative coins.
Download: https://github.com/ckolivas/cgminer

If you want to get a better idea of mining without installing any software, try Bitcoin Plus, a browser-based CPU Bitcoin miner. As a CPU miner it's not cost-efficient for serious mining, but it helps illustrate the process of pool mining.

Into the Cloud. No hardware needed.

I have listed before, several cloud based miners. You pay a fee upfront and depending on the amount of the fee, you are allowed to rent or lease computer power. You are not buying coins. The fees can vary and different companies have contracts that can change in price every few hours. You will most likely rent in GHS or Script speed. The faster your computer power and the longer the contract, the higher your rental costs will be.

Graphic charts:

Difficulty progression continues based on value and use.

You cannot predict the change in difficulty because that is a function of a number of factors that are completely unknowable.

A question that everyone will have sooner or later.

How do we determine the difficulty for mining in the

future?

For example, the difficulty changes because a large number of mining pools suddenly appear and they have very powerful ASICs and a lot of them. How would you ever be able to "predict" this happening?

Another example is the opposite case, that the technology has reached its absolute maximum and there are no new chips yet invented that could give performance boost. Although new miners enter the market, this does not fundamentally change the rate at which the new blocks are discovered, because the chips being used are no more powerful. When we mine for E coins in the cloud, the group we rent from has most likely preselected profitable mining pools. Most of the hard work has already been done for you. A few cloud based miners, do let you select your own pool mining groups, however, I use the default selections. I'm most happy in selecting from a variety of E coins on their list.

Getting started in the cloud, fast and simple.

A good choice in getting started fast and easy is Eobot.com. With their permission, I have included a lot of references directly from their web site for my notes. Customer service is very good. Email support is normally less than 12 hours and the site has a chat feature than has some smart Mods as administrators.

www.Eobot.com

Eobot is the easiest, cheapest, and best way to get or mine Bitcoin,
Litecoin, BlackCoin, Namecoin, Dogecoin, Dash, Reddcoin,
BitSharesX, CureCoin, StorjcoinX, Monero, Counterparty, Stellar,
Paycoin, Peercoin, NXT, and MaidSafeCoin. Whether or not you
use our Cloud Mining or your own hardware, you can mine any
cryptocurrency, regardless if it is based on a SHA-256 or Scrypt
algorithm.

Bitcoin Cloud Mining

Let your computer relax. Our Cloud solution will mine and hash
whatever cryptocurrency you need. Get started with as little as $10
with immediate mining results.

How the Cloud Mining/Hashing Works

- Immediate results, mining updates every 60 seconds
- Can own fractions of cloud instances, if desired
- No heat or hardware to maintain
- Choose payout in any displayed cryptocurrency
- 5 year and 24 hour rental lengths available
- No returns/exchanges
- (Cloud SHA-256) SHA-256 algorithm, 1.0 GHS per 1.0 cloud
instance owned
- (Cloud SHA-256) Follows Bitcoin difficulty, which in the past has

increased exponentially. This means payouts will likely be reduced over time, unless the price of Bitcoin rises to keep pace
- (Cloud Scrypt) Scrypt algorithm, 1.0 KHS per 1.0 cloud instance owned
- (Cloud Scrypt) Follows Litecoin difficulty, which in the past has increased exponentially. This means payouts will likely be reduced over time, unless the price of Litecoin rises to keep pace
- For electricity and maintenance, we take a fee.

Buy Using Cryptocurrency   Buy Using PayPal

Cloud Mining Inventory

SHA-256 5 Year Contracts Sold	SHA-256 Available Total Supply	SHA-256 Ratio
2000 THS	2000 THS	Out of stock No ETA on new arrival 100%

Scrypt 5 Year Contracts Sold	Scrypt Available Total Supply	Scrypt Ratio
3 GHS	3 GHS	Out of stock No ETA on new arrival 100%

Cloud Mining Calculator

Number of GHS (SHA-256)	Number of KHS (Scrypt)	Cryptocurrency	Estimated Mining Payouts*
$0	$0		Daily: 0.00000000 BTC Monthly: 0.00000000 BTC

Examples for Cloud SHA-256 1.0 GHS instance

		Purchase Price	Monthly Mining Payouts*	Mining Break-Even Months*
	USD	$0.25	$0.01	26.60
	BTC	0.0010 BTC	0.0000 BTC	26.60
	LTC	0.1497 LTC	0.0056 LTC	26.60
	BLK	17.0928 BLK	0.6427 BLK	26.60
	NMC	0.6054 NMC	0.0228 NMC	26.60
	DOGE	2012.9497 DOGE	75.6869 DOGE	26.60
	XRP	30.1117 XRP	1.1322 XRP	26.60
	DASH	0.0532 DASH	0.0020 DASH	26.60
	RDD	14739.2578 RDD	554.1961 RDD	26.60
	BTS	38.0502 BTS	1.4307 BTS	26.60
	CURE	28.4523 CURE	1.0698 CURE	26.60
	SJCX	15.1735 SJCX	0.5705 SJCX	26.60

	XMR	0.3537 XMR	0.0133 XMR	26.60
	XCP	0.2059 XCP	0.0077 XCP	26.60
	STR	89.8786 STR	3.3794 STR	26.60
	XPY	0.4457 XPY	0.0168 XPY	26.60
	PPC	0.7756 PPC	0.0292 PPC	26.60
	NXT	24.4834 NXT	0.9206 NXT	26.60
	MAID	12.5840 MAID	0.4732 MAID	26.60

The last column shows the ROI (return on investment as a set value. 3 months ago, my ROI was at 22 months. Currently posted is 26 months on a 5 year contract to break even on rent/leasing high hash rates. Anything past 26 months and you're in the pure profit zone. Unless of course, the difficulty of block mining goes up again and then the ROI will increase to a longer payback time. This should be noted as a sure thing. Difficulty in mining will step up as an increase in computer power is needed and it occurs every few months. Seldom does it decrease, but it does happen. If you started mining 3 years ago with computer graphic cards, your out of luck as computer hash power in using graphics cards can no longer keep up with the latest higher end processers developed only for bitcoin mining. If you're mining in the cloud, your hardware isn't becoming outdated. The cloud miner's players will always offer you the highest computational speed available at a premium price of course.

Let not forget this part of all Cloud mining contracts is the notice of risk.

*Cloud mining should be considered as a fun, recreational activity and not a source of income or investment. The above numbers reflect no difficulty increase. Investing involves risk, including possible loss of principal.

In addition to the normal risks associated with investing and mining, cryptocurrency mining investments and related instruments may involve risk of capital loss from unfavorable fluctuation in cryptocurrency values, exchange-related risks, policy risks, liquidity, and market price fluctuation and demand.

The strategies discussed are strictly for illustrative and educational purposes and should not be construed as a recommendation to purchase. There is no guarantee that any strategies discussed will be effective. The information provided is not intended to be a complete analysis of every material fact respecting any strategy. The examples presented do not take into consideration commissions, tax implications, or other transactions costs, which may significantly affect the economic consequences of a given strategy.
Fiat amounts (real money value) shown are the equivalents if cryptocurrency is traded on the popular exchanges, such as Cryptsy. Eobot does not allow fiat (USD/EUR/JPY/GBP/CNY/RUB/etc.) in or out. Fiat amounts are for illustrative purposes only.
Eobot has no opinion regarding alleged relative values of virtual

currencies in relation to fiat currencies.

If you download and use EoBot software for use on your computer hardware or graphics card, please be aware of these values. Its value per month is set in bitcoins. Doesn't include any electrical cost where you live. That's why I use the cloud service since I work and live in Hawaii USA, it's more cost effective for me not to worry about hardware issues, internet connections

and power costs. I'm 100% mining in the cloud. Listed below are the approximate profits you might expect less electric costs.

Current difficulty in Steps. Notice that on rare occasions, it can decrease, but it's rare.

http://bitcoin.sipa.be/

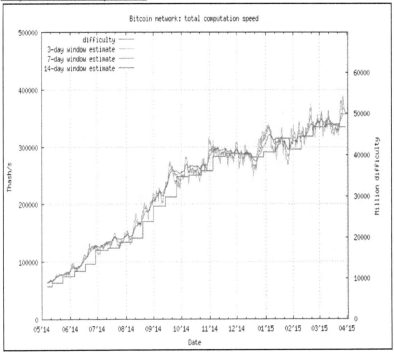

https://cryptracer.com/

Cryptrader has some of the most amazing and flexible charting options if you need some short or long term referencing for which direction the market may be heading. See the charts below.

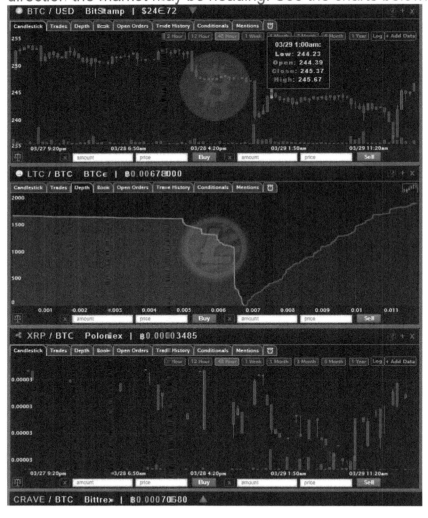

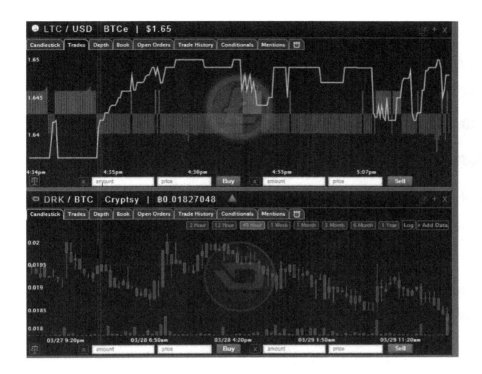

Making Money

Approximate Rates When

Using Software on your PC

High End Gaming Machine (e.g. two high end Radeon cards) ~ 0.014 BTC a month
Low End Gaming Machine (e.g. one mid range Radeon card) ~ 0.007 BTC a month
High End Server/Laptop (no graphics card, uses CPU mode) ~ 0.00005 BTC a month
Low End Server/Laptop (no graphics card, uses CPU mode) ~ 0.00001 BTC a month

With the above approximate rates, calculate for example Bitcoin price times 0.014 BTC a month for the high end gaming machine with 2 high end graphic cards that would cost around $400 each. We will use a simple average price of $250 per bitcoin to get started. Your profit would be as listed:

$250 BTC * 0.014 a month= $3.50

Electrical power costs will run about 75% of those profits.

$3.50 -$2.62=$0.88 a month

Yes, that's right 0.88 cents a month or 0.0293 cents per day on a 30 day month average.

As you can tell from these simple calculations, you're going to have to have some heavy duty computer power to make any money.

In the screen shot below is my live account, mining in the Eobot cloud. At this time, there are 20 different coins you can mine for at any time, 24 hrs. a day, 7 days a week. You can even diversify and select more than one coin. On occasion I will diversify and mine 2 or more coins. The EoBot web site will automatically make these changes for you and will change to your coin selection on a rotating time limit of one minute each. If you select 8 coins, it will mine each coin for one minute and then change to the next one you have selected. At the bottom of your front page is a graph. Here's how mine looks at this time. I trade these 2 coins primarily. BTC and DASH (formaly called Dark Coin).

At my current speed of 800 GHS, I'm making around 0.015

cents per hour (USD) or 0.36 cents a day. That's $10.80 USD a month. At the price I leased at, that's around $200, and it's a full 5 year contract. To make around $100 a month for 5 years, you will need $2000 for increased Hashing power leasing/rental. Not including the increase in the difficulty level of mining in the next five years. Remember, it's not an investment; you are contributing your cash into computer Hashing power/leasing for 5 years, to do cryptocurrency mining.

BTC
DASH
Other

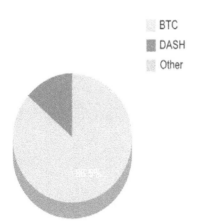

Garry H.'s Profile

Total Cryptocurrency Value $ 2.01138854

Bitcoin
0.00713232 BTC
$ 243.5+
$ 1.73985804

Litecoin
0.00000000 LTC
$ 1.6?
$ 0.000#001

BlackCoin
0.00000000 BLK
$ 0.015
$ 0.00000000

Namecoin
0.00000000 NMC
$ 0.41
$ 0.00000000

Dogecoin
9.00000001 DOGE
$ 0.00013
$ 0.00113943

Ripple
0.00000000 XRP
$ 0.808
$ 0.00000000

Dash
0.05848082 DASH
$ 4.6
$ 0.2694:245

Reddcoin
0.00000000 RDD
$ 0.00002
$ 0.00000000

BitSharesX
0.00000000 BTS
$ 0.007
$ 0.00000000

CureCoin
0.00000000 CURE
$ 0.009
$ 0.00000000

Storjcoin X
0.00000000 SJCX
$ 0.017
$ 0.000#0000

Monero
0.00000000 XMR
$ 0.7?
$ 0.000#000

Counterparty
0.00000000 XCP
$ 1.21
$ 0.00000000

Stellar
0.00000000 STR
$ 0.003
$ 0.00000000

Paycoin
0.00000000 XPY
$ 0.57
$ 0.00000000

Peercoin
0.00000000 PPC
$ 0.32
$ 0.0000000

NXT
0.00000000 NXT
$ 0.01#
$ 0.0000000

MaidSafeCoin
0.04980209 MAID
$ 0.020
$ 0.00098860

Cloud Folding
0.00000000 PPD
$ 0.06

Cloud Mining
80.93961060 GHS
$ 0.25
0.00000000   KHS
$ 0.01

A few more online references:

http://cloudminingdirectory.com/faqs/

http://en.m.wikipedia.org/wiki/Bitcoin

http://www.butterflylabs.com/bitcoin-mining/

http://www.bitcoinmining.com/bitcoin-mining-hardware/

https://www.weusecoins.com/en/mining-guide

http://www.bitcoinmining.com/bitcoin-mining-software/

http://www.eobot.com/

https://bitcoinmagazine.com/

http://bitcoin.sipa.be/

https://cryptrader.com/

If you're interested in mining for bitcoins of any type, consider cryptocurrency/e-coin, mining in the cloud. It's a risk for sure, but it's a lot of fun. And your mining can begin within 3 minutes or less after you register for free online. Many other types of Cloud based mining are coming online each month. Read my notes and follow the links I have provided for you. Garry's Notes, should help you make an informed choice. Good luck, and God Bless.

Sincerely

Garry Higgins

PS.

Im also the author of Quail Notes.

QUAIL
N O T E S

**Raising Quail For Fun Or Profit
Sharing My Story Of Raising Quail
On The Back Porch Or On The Farm.**

By Garry D Higgins

Raising Quail at home for fun and profit. It's also available
on Amazon.com or other book stores as a e book for $2.99
or in print for $5.99